My Most Beautiful Dream

Mi sueño más bonito

Bilingual children's picture book, with audiobook for download

Audiobook and video:

www.sefa-bilingual.com/bonus

Password for free access:

English: **BDEN1423**

Spanish: **BDES1428**

Cornelia Haas · Ulrich Renz

My Most Beautiful Dream

Mi sueño más bonito

Bilingual children's picture book,

with audiobook for download

Translation:

Sefâ Jesse Konuk Agnew (English)

Raquel Catala (Spanish)

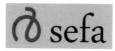

Lulu can't fall asleep. Everyone else is dreaming already – the shark, the elephant, the little mouse, the dragon, the kangaroo, the knight, the monkey, the pilot. And the lion cub. Even the bear has trouble keeping his eyes open ...

Hey bear, will you take me along into your dream?

Lulu no puede dormir. Todos los demás ya están soñando – el tiburón, el elefante, el ratoncito, el dragón, el canguro, el caballero, el mono, el piloto. Y el pequeño leoncito. Al osito también se le cierran casi los ojos ...

Oye osito, ¿me llevas contigo a tu sueño?

And with that, Lulu finds herself in bear dreamland. The bear catches fish in Lake Tagayumi. And Lulu wonders, who could be living up there in the trees?

When the dream is over, Lulu wants to go on another adventure. Come along, let's visit the shark! What could he be dreaming?

Y así está Lulu en el país de los sueños de los osos. El osito está pescando en el lago de Tagayumi. Y Lulu se pregunta, ¿quién vivirá arriba en los árboles?

Al terminar el sueño, Lulu quiere descubrir aún măs cosas. ¡Ven con nosotros, vamos a visitar al tiburón! ¿Qué estará soñando?

The shark plays tag with the fish. Finally he's got some friends! Nobody's afraid of his sharp teeth.

When the dream is over, Lulu wants to go on another adventure. Come along, let's visit the elephant! What could he be dreaming?

El tiburón está jugando a perseguir a los peces. ¡Por fin tiene amigos! Nadie tiene miedo de sus dientes puntiagudos.

Al terminar el sueño, Lulu quiere descubrir aún más cosas. ¡Venid con nosotros, vamos a visitar al elefante! ¿Qué estará soñando?

The elephant is as light as a feather and can fly! He's about to land on the celestial meadow.

When the dream is over, Lulu wants to go on another adventure. Come along, let's visit the little mouse! What could she be dreaming?

El elefante es tan ligero como una pluma y ¡puede volar! Está a punto de aterrizar en la pradera celestial.

Al terminar el sueño, Lulu quiere descubrir aún más cosas. ¡Venid con nosotros, vamos a visitar al ratoncito! ¿Qué estará soñando?

The little mouse watches the fair. She likes the roller coaster best.
When the dream is over, Lulu wants to go on another adventure. Come
along, let's visit the dragon! What could she be dreaming?

El ratoncito está mirando la feria. Lo que más le gusta es la montaña rusa. Al terminar el sueño, Lulu quiere descubrir aún más cosas. ¡Venid con nosotros, vamos a visitar al dragón! ¿Qué estará soñando?

The dragon is thirsty from spitting fire. She'd like to drink up the whole lemonade lake.

When the dream is over, Lulu wants to go on another adventure. Come along, let's visit the kangaroo! What could she be dreaming?

El dragón tiene sed de tanto escupir fuego. Le gustaría beberse todo el lago de limonada.

Al terminar el sueño, Lulu quiere descubrir aún más cosas. ¡Venid con nosotros, vamos a visitar al canguro! ¿Qué estará soñando?

The kangaroo jumps around the candy factory and fills her pouch. Even more of the blue sweets! And more lollipops! And chocolate!

When the dream is over, Lulu wants to go on another adventure. Come along, let's visit the knight! What could he be dreaming?

El canguro salta por la fábrica de dulces y llena toda su bolsa. ¡Más de los caramelos azules! ¡Y más piruletas! ¡Y chocolate!

Al terminar el sueño, Lulu quiere descubrir aún más cosas. ¡Venid con nosotros, vamos a visitar al caballero! ¿Qué estará soñando?

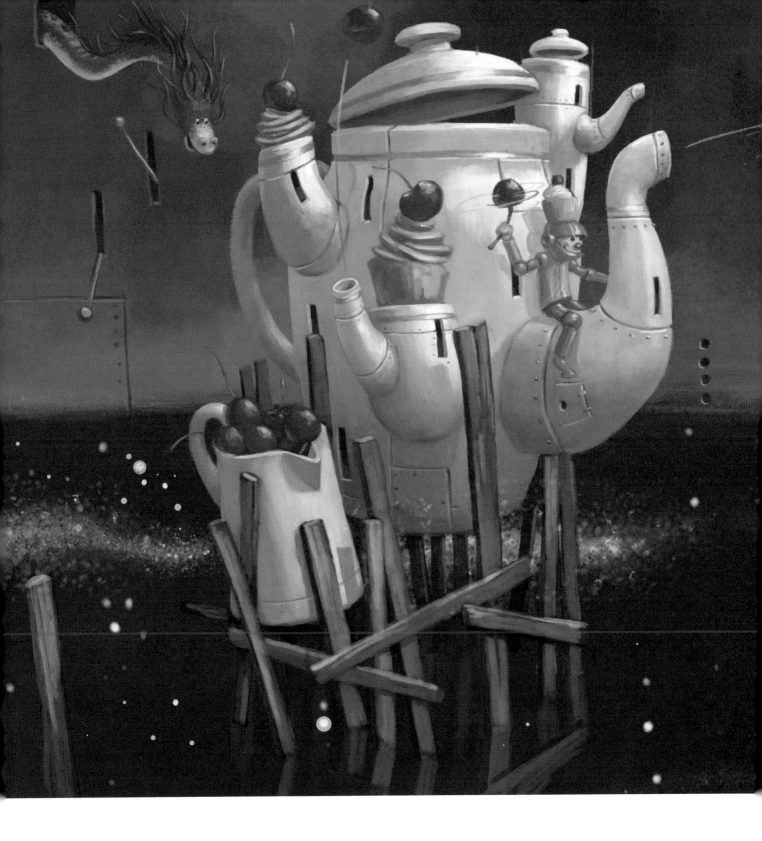

The knight is having a cake fight with his dream princess. Oops! The whipped cream cake has gone the wrong way!

When the dream is over, Lulu wants to go on another adventure. Come along, let's visit the monkey! What could he be dreaming?

El caballero está teniendo una pelea de pasteles con la princesa de sus
sueños. ¡Oh, no! ¡El pastel de crema ha ido en la dirección equivocada!
Al terminar el sueño, Lulu quiere descubrir aún más cosas. ¡Venid con
nosotros, vamos a visitar al mono! ¿Qué estará soñando?

Snow has finally fallen in Monkeyland. The whole barrel of monkeys is beside itself and getting up to monkey business.

When the dream is over, Lulu wants to go on another adventure. Come along, let's visit the pilot! In which dream could he have landed?

¡Por fin ha nevado en el país de los monos! Toda la banda de monos se ha vuelto loca y está haciendo tonterías.

Al terminar el sueño, Lulu quiere descubrir aún más cosas. ¡Venid con nosotros, vamos a visitar al piloto! ¿En qué sueño habrá aterrizado?

The pilot flies on and on. To the ends of the earth, and even farther, right on up to the stars. No other pilot has ever managed that.

When the dream is over, everybody is very tired and doesn't feel like going on many adventures anymore. But they'd still like to visit the lion cub.

What could she be dreaming?

El piloto vuela y vuela. Hasta el fin del mundo y aún más allá, hasta las estrellas. Esto no lo ha conseguido ningún otro piloto.

Al terminar el sueño, están ya todos muy cansados y no desean descubrir mucho más. Pero aún quieren visitar al pequeño leoncito. ¿Qué estará soñando?

The lion cub is homesick and wants to go back to the warm, cozy bed.
And so do the others.

And thus begins ...

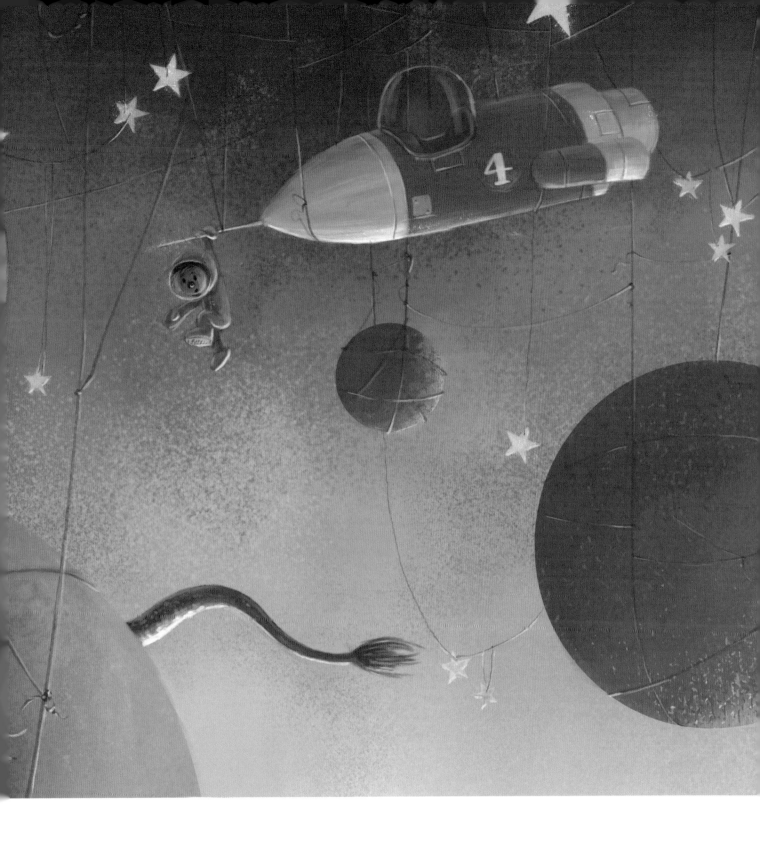

El pequeño leoncito tiene nostalgia y quiere volver a su cálida y acogedora cama.

Y los demás también.

Y ahí empieza ...

... Lulu's
most beautiful dream.

... el sueño más bonito
de Lulu.

Foto: Ingrid Hagenreich

Cornelia Haas was born near Augsburg, Germany, in 1972. After completing her apprenticeship as a sign and light advertising manufacturer, she studied design at the Münster University of Applied Sciences and graduated with a degree in design. Since 2001 she has been illustrating childrens' and adolescents' books, since 2013 she has been teaching acrylic and digital painting at the Münster University of Applied Sciences.

Cornelia Haas nació en 1972 cerca de Augsburg, Alemania. Después de su formación como fabricante de cárteles publicitarios, estudió diseño en la escuela técnica superior en Münster y allí se graduó como diseñadora. Desde 2001 ha ilustrado libros infantiles y juveniles, desde 2013 enseña como profesora de pintura acrílica y digital en la escuela técnica superior de Münster.

www.cornelia-haas.de

Do you like drawing?

Here are the pictures from the story to color in:

www.sefa-bilingual.com/coloring

Enjoy!

Dear Reader,

Thanks for choosing my book! If you (and most of all, your child) liked it, please spread the word via a Facebook-Like or an email to your friends:

www.sefa-bilingual.com/like

I would also be happy to get a comment or a review. Likes and comments are great „Tender Loving Care" for authors, thanks so much!

If there is no audiobook version in your language yet, please be patient! We are working on making all the languages available as audiobooks. You can check the „Language Wizard" for the latest updates:

www.sefa-bilingual.com/languages

Now let me briefly introduce myself: I was born in Stuttgart in 1960, together with my twin brother Herbert (who also became a writer). I studied French literature and a couple of languages in Paris, then medicine in Lübeck. However, my career as a doctor was brief because I soon discovered books: medical books at first, for which I was an editor and a publisher, and later non-fiction and children's books.

I live with my wife Kirsten in Lübeck in the very north of Germany; together we have three (now grown) children, a dog, two cats, and a little publishing house: Sefa Press.

If you want to know more about me, you are welcome to visit my website: **www.ulrichrenz.de**

Best regards,

Ulrich Renz

Lulu also recommends:

Tim can't fall asleep. His little wolf is missing! Perhaps he forgot him outside?
Tim heads out all alone into the night – and unexpectedly encounters some friends ...

Available in your languages?

► Check out with our „Language Wizard":

www.sefa-bilingual.com/languages

Ulrich Renz · Marc Robitzky

The Wild Swans
Los cisnes salvajes

Based on a fairy tale by

Hans Christian Andersen

+ audio   + video

English   bilingual   Spanish

The Wild Swans

Based on a fairy tale by Hans Christian Andersen

Recommended age: 4-5 and up

with online audio and video

„The Wild Swans" by Hans Christian Andersen is, with good reason, one of the world's most popular fairy tales. In its timeless form it addresses the issues out of which human dramas are made: fear, bravery, love, betrayal, separation and reunion.

Available in your languages?

▶ Check out with our „Language Wizard":

www.sefa-bilingual.com/languages

More of me ...

Bo & Friends

► Children's detective series in three volumes. Reading age: 9+

► German Edition: „Motte & Co" ► www.motte-und-co.de

► Download the series' first volume, „Bo and the Blackmailers" for free!

www.bo-and-friends.com/free

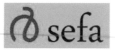

IT: Paul Bödeker, Freiburg, Germany

ISBN: 9783739960296

Version: 20190101

www.sefa-bilingual.com

Printed in Great Britain
by Amazon

79562271R00025